INDIAN COOKBOOK

40 Delicious & Healthy Recipes

Ella Porter

Table of Contents

__INTRODUCTION__

I want to thank you and congratulate you for downloading the "Indian Cookbook"

It's the time to have some Indian recipes which are amazingly delicious and taken from the taste of India. This eBook is all about easy and extremely tempting Indian recipes traditional and contemporary so that you can explore the classic and innovative Indian taste, at the same time. Make your occasions and festivals filled with sweet memories and smiles through this exclusively compiled recipe collection. Whether it's a Diwali or Eid, New Year party or Birthday occasion, you would find this book the ultimate Indian recipes collection, to please your friends, family, and guests.

Indian food is a mixture of spices and various ingredients, which makes it a unique cuisine with some world-famous recipes. Many people have a misconception of Indian food being complicated, which is nothing more than a myth. Flavor rich food can be easily prepared at home with just a few steps. Most of the recipes can be prepared with 15 to 25 minutes by inexperienced cooks. This Indian cookbook will make you want to have Indian food every day.

This cookbook contains 40 hand-picked recipes with easy to follow instructions. Explore dedicated sections on popular breakfasts, dinner, snack, side, salad, and desserts celebrating the true spirit of Indian cuisines.

❖ Spice Indian Foods:

Spices do not necessarily mean adding more heat to your foods; popular Indian spices make their recipes scrumptious.

- **Black pepper:**

These originated from India specifically from Malabar and Western Ghats. The flavor is a beast when freshly ground.

- **Cumin Seeds:**

Cumin seeds are quite essential to Indian food. Not only are they great digestion facilitator, but they are also immunity boosters.

- **Cardamom:**

Green cardamom is most commonly used in Indian cuisines. It has a sweetish taste with a touch of eucalyptus.

- **Chaat Masala:**

Chaat masala is made from dried mango powder, dried ginger, coriander, black salt, red pepper, asafetida, black pepper, black salt, and salt. This sprinkled over dishes after cooking.

- **Black Mustard Seeds:**

Black mustard seeds make recipes truly appetizing and irresistible.

- **Asafetida:**

It has a mild fragrance, however; it contains super flavor boosting capacity.

- **Coriander powder:**

Coriander adds freshness to food and it is packed with health benefits including preventing inflammation, indigestion and high cholesterol level.

BREAKFAST RECIPES
1-Tasty Masala Toast

Time: 20 minutes

Serve: 2

Ingredients:

- 3 bread slices
- 2 green chilies, chopped
- 1 onion, chopped
- 1/4 tsp black pepper
- 1 tbsp fresh coriander, chopped
- 1 tbsp red chili flakes
- 2 tbsp milk
- 4 eggs
- 2 tbsp olive oil
- Salt

Directions:

- Beat eggs into the bowl with black pepper, chili flakes, milk, and salt.
- Heat oil in a pan over medium heat.
- Dip bread slices into the egg mixture then place on hot pan.
- Spread chopped coriander, green chilies, and onion on top of bread then pour some egg mixture on it.
- Flip the bread and let cook the other side.
- Once it looks lightly golden brown then removes from pan and serve.

Nutritional Value (Amount per Serving):

- Calories 336
- Fat 23.8 g
- Carbohydrates 19.1 g
- Sugar 7.1 g
- Protein 14.3 g
- Cholesterol 329 mg

2-Indian Lemon Quinoa Breakfast

Time: 20 minutes

Serve: 2

Ingredients:

- 1/2 cup quinoa, rinsed, drained and cooked
- 2 tbsp oil
- 1/4 tsp ground turmeric
- 1 red chili, dried
- 2 green chilies
- 4 curry leaves
- 2 tbsp cashew nuts
- 2 tbsp peanuts
- 1/2 tsp chana dal
- 1/2 tsp urad dal
- 3/4 tsp mustard seeds

- 2 tbsp lemon juice
- Salt

Directions:

- Heat oil in pan over medium heat.
- Once oil is hot then add chana dal, urad dal, mustard seeds, and peanuts and sauté until chana dal become lightly brown.
- Add cashews and sauté until lightly golden brown.
- Add curry leaves, red chili, and green chilies and sauté for minute.
- Add ground turmeric and sauté for seconds.
- Now add cooked quinoa and salt and stir well.
- Remove from heat and add lemon juice.
- Stir well and serve.

Nutritional Value (Amount per Serving):

- Calories 436
- Fat 25.6 g
- Carbohydrates 43.3 g
- Sugar 7.1 g
- Protein 12.1 g
- Cholesterol 0 mg

3-Indian Breakfast Pancake

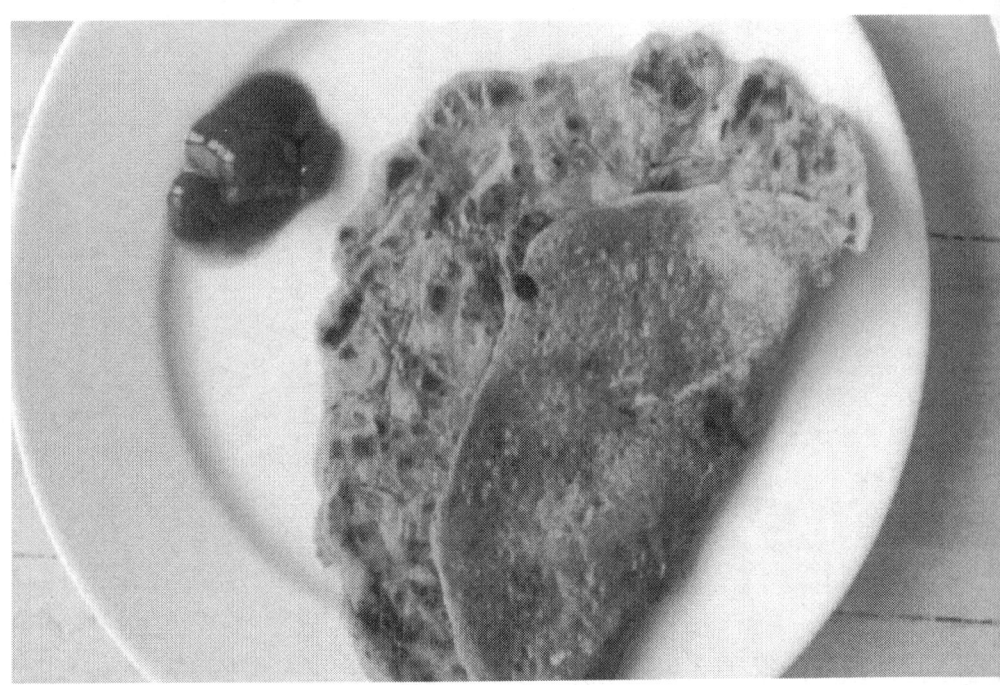

Time: 25 minutes

Serve: 4

Ingredients:

- 2 cups gram flour
- 4 tsp oil
- 2 tbsp fresh coriander, chopped
- 1 green chili, chopped
- 1 tsp coriander powder
- 1 tsp red chili powder
- 2/3 cup broccoli, grated
- 1/4 onion, chopped
- 1 cup water
- Salt

Directions:

- In a large bowl, mix together gram flour, turmeric powder, coriander powder, vegetables, red chili powder, and salt.
- Pour enough water into the bowl mixture to make medium thick pouring consistency.
- Whisk batter well and set aside for 10 minutes.
- Grease pan with oil and heat over medium heat.
- Once pan is hot then pour 1/4 cup batter on hot pan and spread evenly in round shape.
- When pancake edges become lightly golden brown then flip the pancake to other side and cook until lightly golden brown.
- Serve hot with ketchup and enjoy.

Nutritional Value (Amount per Serving):

- Calories 234
- Fat 7.8 g
- Carbohydrates 30 g
- Sugar 6.3 g
- Protein 11.2 g
- Cholesterol 0 mg

4-Yummy Potato Sandwich

Time: 20 minutes

Serve: 2

Ingredients:

- 4 bread slices
- 2 tsp butter, melted
- For sandwich filling:
- 2 tsp oil
- 1/2 tsp cumin seeds
- 1/4 tsp chaat masala powder
- 1/2 tsp turmeric powder
- 1/2 tsp pepper powder
- 1/2 tsp cumin powder
- 1/8 cup green peas
- 1 large potato, boiled, peeled and mashed

Directions:

- Heat oil in pan over medium heat.
- Once oil is hot then add cumin seed in hot oil and let them crackle.
- Add green peas and sauté for minutes or until soften.
- Add mashed potato, all spice and salt and stir well to combine and cook for 5 minutes.
- Take bread slices and cut the edges.
- Apply butter on bread slices.
- Spread 3 tbsp potato mixture on one bread slice then cover with another slice.
- Repeat same with remaining two bread slices.
- Toast sandwich in sandwich maker until crisp.
- Serve and enjoy.

Nutritional Value (Amount per Serving):

- Calories 277
- Fat 9.4 g
- Carbohydrates 43.5 g
- Sugar 2.8 g
- Protein 5.9 g
- Cholesterol 10 mg

5-Vegeatble Bread Upma

Time: 20 minutes

Serve: 3

Ingredients:

- 6 bread slices, torn into pieces
- 3 tsp oil
- 1/2 tbsp lemon juice
- 1/2 tsp cumin seeds
- 2 green pepper, slit
- 1/2 tsp ginger, grated
- 1 medium onion, chopped
- 1/2 red bell pepper, chopped
- 1/2 green bell pepper, chopped
- 2 baby corns, chopped
- 1 small carrot, peeled and chopped
- Salt

Directions:

- Heat oil in pan over medium heat.
- Once oil is hot then add cumin seeds and let it crackle.
- Add ginger and green pepper and sauté for 2 minutes.
- Add chopped onion and sauté until soften.
- Add chopped vegetables and sauté for minutes.
- Add turmeric and salt and mix well.
- Add 1/8 cup water and cook the vegetables.
- Add bread pieces and mix well.
- Remove from heat and add lemon juice.
- Stir well and serve hot.

Nutritional Value (Amount per Serving):

- Calories 227
- Fat 6.7 g
- Carbohydrates 40 g
- Sugar 9.9 g
- Protein 6.4 g
- Cholesterol 0 mg

6-Egg Bhurji

Time: 20 minutes

Serve: 2

Ingredients:

- 3 eggs
- 1 tbsp fresh coriander, chopped
- 2 tbsp oil
- 1/2 tsp turmeric powder
- 1 tsp coriander powder
- 1 tsp chili powder
- 1 green chili, slit
- 1 large onion, sliced
- Salt

Directions:

- Heat oil in pan over medium heat.
- Add onion and chili and sauté until lightly brown.
- Add coriander powder, chili powder, and turmeric and stir well.
- Add coriander leaves and eggs and stir until egg cooked.
- Stir well to break egg mixture.
- Serve hot and enjoy.

Nutritional Value (Amount per Serving):

- Calories 251
- Fat 20.5 g
- Carbohydrates 8.6 g
- Sugar 3.8 g
- Protein 9.3 g
- Cholesterol 246 mg

7-Delicious Paneer Bhurji

Time: 20 minutes

Serve: 3

Ingredients:

- 1 cup paneer, grated
- 1/2 tbsp oil
- 4 tbsp milk
- 1/4 tsp kasuri methi
- 1/2 tsp coriander powder
- 1/8 tsp cumin powder
- 1/4 tsp red chili powder
- 1/8 tsp turmeric powder
- 1 tomato, chopped
- 1 green chili, chopped
- 1 onion, chopped

- Salt

Directions:

- Heat oil in pan over medium heat.
- Add green chili and onion and sauté until soften.
- Add kasuri methi, chili powder, coriander powder, cumin powder, salt and turmeric powder and stir well.
- Add chopped tomato and cook for 4 minutes.
- Add grated paneer and stir to combine and cook for 3 minutes.
- Add milk and toss well over medium high heat.
- Serve hot and enjoy.

Nutritional Value (Amount per Serving):

- Calories 86
- Fat 2.9 g
- Carbohydrates 10.3 g
- Sugar 8.4 g
- Protein 4.7 g
- Cholesterol 4 mg

8-Crispy Semolina Toast

Time: 25 minutes

Serve: 2

Ingredients:

- 4 bread slices
- 2 tbsp fresh coriander, chopped
- 2 tbsp yogurt
- 1/2 tsp red chili powder
- 1 green chili, chopped
- 1/4 cup bell pepper, chopped
- 1/2 tsp ginger, grated
- 1/2 tsp cumin seeds
- 1/4 cup onion, chopped
- 1/2 cup semolina
- Oil

- Salt

Directions:

- Add all ingredients except oil and bread into the bowl and mix well then add water and make thick batter.
- Spread batter over one side of bread slice.
- Heat little oil in pan over medium heat.
- Once pan is hot then place bread slice on pan, batter side down and cook until lightly golden brown.
- Flip bread slice and cook until crisp.
- Cut into triangles and serve.

Nutritional Value (Amount per Serving):

- Calories 225
- Fat 1.5 g
- Carbohydrates 44 g
- Sugar 3.3 g
- Protein 8.1 g
- Cholesterol 1 mg

9-Masala Omelette

Time: 10 minutes

Serve: 1

Ingredients:

- 2 eggs
- 1/4 tsp red chili powder
- 1/8 tsp turmeric powder
- 1 tbsp fresh coriander, chopped
- 1 tbsp green bell pepper, chopped
- 1 tbsp tomato, chopped
- 2 tbsp onion, chopped
- 2 tbsp milk
- 1 tsp oil
- Salt

Directions:

- Break in mixing bowl and whisk well.
- Add remaining ingredients except oil and whisk well.
- Heat oil in pan over medium heat.
- Pour egg mixture on pan and spread evenly.
- Once omelet edges looks lightly golden brown then flip and cook for minutes.
- Serve and enjoy.

Nutritional Value (Amount per Serving):

- Calories 232
- Fat 14.4 g
- Carbohydrates 14.1 g
- Sugar 9.3 g
- Protein 13.7 g
- Cholesterol 330 mg

10-Flattened Rice with Yogurt

Time: 15 minutes

Serve: 2

Ingredients:

- 1 cup flattened rice
- 2 tsp oil
- 3 tbsp pomegranate seeds
- 4 curry leaves
- 1/2 tsp cumin seeds
- 1/4 tsp mustard seeds
- 1/2 tsp ginger, grated
- 2 green chilies, chopped
- 2 1/2 cups yogurt
- Salt

Directions:

- Rinse flattened rice and drain well. Set aside for 5 minutes.
- Add salt in yogurt and beat until smooth.
- Add flattened rice into the yogurt and mix well and set aside for 10 minutes.
- For tempering heat oil in small saucepan.
- Once oil is hot then add mustard seeds and let them splutter.
- Add cumin seeds and stir once and let them crackle.
- Add green chilies, ginger, and curry leaves and sauté for minutes.
- Add seasoning to the prepared flattened rice and mix well.
- Garnish with pomegranate seeds and serve.

Nutritional Value (Amount per Serving):

- Calories 573
- Fat 12.1 g
- Carbohydrates 63.8 g
- Sugar 41.6 g
- Protein 25.2 g
- Cholesterol 18 mg

DINNER RECIPES
11-Delicious Butter Chicken

Time: 40 minutes

Serve: 4

Ingredients:

- 1 1/2 lbs chicken thighs, boneless and skinless
- 1 cup heavy cream
- 1 tbsp white granulated sugar
- 1 cup tomato puree
- 1 tbsp vegetable oil
- 1 tsp garlic, minced
- 1/2 tbsp ginger paste
- 1 tsp ground cumin
- 1/2 tsp chili powder
- 2 tsp garam masala

- 1 tsp turmeric powder
- 1 tbsp lemon juice
- 1/2 cup sour cream
- 1 tsp salt
- Pepper

Directions:

- Season chicken with pepper and salt and set aside.
- In a bowl, combine together garlic, ginger paste, cumin, chili powder, garam masala, turmeric, lemon juice, and sour cream, and toss with chicken.
- Cover bowl and place in refrigerator for 1 hour.
- Heat oil in a pan over medium high heat.
- Add marinated chicken on pan and cook for 5 minutes.
- Add sugar, salt and tomato puree. Stir well.
- Turn heat to low and cover pan with lid.
- Let the simmer for 20 minutes.
- Add cream and stir well.
- Serve hot and enjoy.

Nutritional Value (Amount per Serving):

- Calories 551
- Fat 33.6 g
- Carbohydrates 9.3 g
- Sugar 3.3 g
- Protein 52.1 g
- Cholesterol 205 mg

12-Coconut Lentil Curry

Time: 50 minutes

Serve: 6

Ingredients:

- 1 cup brown lentils, dried
- 1 cup cilantro, chopped
- 15 oz can coconut milk
- 1 tbsp turmeric
- 2 tbsp ginger, chopped
- 28 oz can tomatoes, crushed
- 3 garlic cloves, chopped
- 1 tbsp coriander seeds
- 1 tbsp cumin seeds
- 2 tbsp coconut oil
- 1/4 cup cherry tomatoes

- 2 tsp sea salt

Directions:

- Heat coconut oil in a pot over medium high heat.
- Add coriander seeds and cumin and stir for 45 seconds.
- Add garlic and sauté for 2 minutes.
- Add turmeric, ginger, can tomatoes, and sea salt. Stir well and cook for 5 minutes.
- Add lentils and 3 cups water and bring to boil.
- Reduce heat to low and simmer for 35 minutes.
- Stir well to prevent sticking.
- Once lentils are soften then add cherry tomatoes and coconut milk. Stir well and bring the pot back to simmer for minutes.
- Remove from heat and stir well.
- Garnish with cilantro and serve hot.

Nutritional Value (Amount per Serving):

- Calories 273
- Fat 13.6 g
- Carbohydrates 31.6 g
- Sugar 3.9 g
- Protein 10.8 g
- Cholesterol 0 mg

13-Delicious Vegetarian Korma

Time: 35 minutes

Serve: 4

Ingredients:

- 1 cup coconut milk, unsweetened
- 1/2 red bell pepper, chopped
- 1/2 green bell pepper, chopped
- 1 cup green peas
- 2 tbsp curry powder
- 1/2 cup tomato sauce
- 3 tbsp cashews, crushed
- 4 carrots, chopped
- 3 potatoes, cubed
- 5 garlic cloves, minced
- 1 tsp ginger, grated

- 1 small onion, diced
- 2 tbsp olive oil
- 2 tsp salt

Directions:

- Heat olive oil in a pan over medium heat.
- Add onion and sauté until tender.
- Add garlic and ginger and sauté for minutes.
- Add tomato sauce, cashews, carrots, and potatoes and mix well.
- Season with curry powder and salt.
- Stir well and cook for 15 minutes or until potatoes are tender.
- Stir coconut milk, red bell pepper, green bell pepper, and peas into the pan.
- Reduce heat to low. Cover and simmer for 10 minutes.
- Serve hot with rice and enjoy.

Nutritional Value (Amount per Serving):

- Calories 442
- Fat 25.3 g
- Carbohydrates 51 g
- Sugar 12.9 g
- Protein 9.2 g
- Cholesterol 0 mg

14-Chickpea Curry

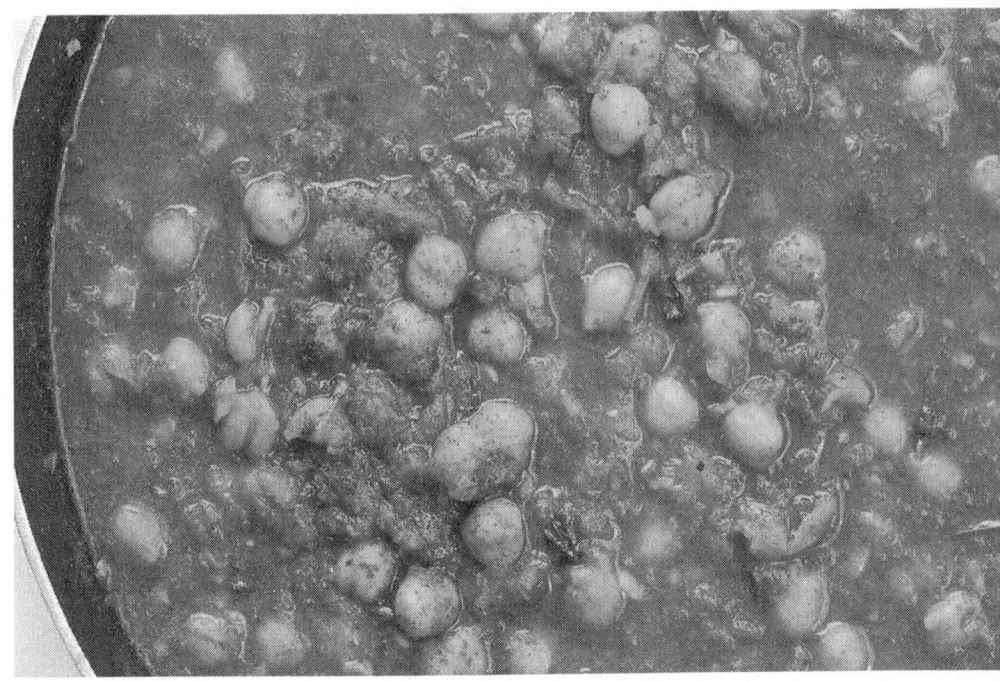

Time: 30 minutes

Serve: 8

Ingredients:

- 15 oz can chickpeas, drained and rinsed
- 1 tsp cornstarch
- 13 oz can coconut milk
- 14 oz can tomatoes, diced
- 1/2 tsp cayenne pepper
- 1 tsp turmeric
- 3 tsp ground coriander
- 2 tsp ground cumin
- 1 tbsp garam masala
- 1 tsp ginger, grated
- 2 garlic cloves, minced

- 1 large onion, chopped
- 2 tbsp olive oil
- Salt

Directions:

- Heat olive oil in saucepan over medium high heat.
- Add onion and salt and sauté for 5 minutes.
- Add garlic and sauté for 1 minute.
- Add ginger and spices and sauté for 30 seconds.
- Add tomatoes and chickpeas and stir well. Bring to boil.
- Reduce heat to low and simmer for 15 minutes.
- Stir in coconut milk and simmer for 5 minutes.
- In small bowl, whisk together 2 tbsp water and cornstarch.
- Stir in chickpea mixture and cook for 5 minutes or until thicken.
- Taste curry and adjust seasoning.
- Serve hot and enjoy.

Nutritional Value (Amount per Serving):

- Calories 209
- Fat 14.1 g
- Carbohydrates 18.8 g
- Sugar 2.5 g
- Protein 4.4 g
- Cholesterol 0 mg

15-Stir Fried Cabbage

Time: 20 minutes

Serve: 4

Ingredients:

- 1 cabbage head, shredded
- 3/4 cup fresh green peas
- 1 tbsp coriander powder
- 1 tsp paprika powder
- 1 tsp ginger, grated
- 1 tsp cumin seeds
- 2 tbsp oil
- Salt

Directions:

- Heat oil in pan over medium heat.

- Add cumin and ginger and sauté for minute.
- Add coriander powder, paprika, cabbage, and salt and mix well.
- Add 1/4 cup water and cover pan and cook for 10 minutes.
- Add green peas and cook for minute.
- Serve hot and enjoy.

Nutritional Value (Amount per Serving):

- Calories 130
- Fat 7.2 g
- Carbohydrates 14.8 g
- Sugar 7.3 g
- Protein 3.9 g
- Cholesterol 0 mg

16-Potato Cauliflower Curry

Time: 25 minutes

Serve: 2

Ingredients:

- 3 cups cauliflower florets, cut into 1 inch pieces
- 2 cups potatoes, peeled and cubed
- 3 tbsp water
- 3 tbsp oil
- 1/2 tsp cayenne
- 3 tsp curry powder
- 1 tbsp lemon juice
- 3/4 cup frozen peas
- 1 tsp salt

Directions:

- Heat oil in pan over medium heat.
- Add potatoes and sauté for minute.
- Add cauliflower and sauté for another minute.
- Add cayenne powder, curry powder, water, and salt. Stir well.
- Reduce heat to low. Cover and cook for 10 minutes.
- Add peas and set heat medium high. Stir well and cook for 2 minutes.
- Remove from heat and add lemon juice. Stir well.
- Serve immediately and enjoy.

Nutritional Value (Amount per Serving):

- Calories 381
- Fat 21.4 g
- Carbohydrates 42.2 g
- Sugar 8.4 g
- Protein 9.1 g
- Cholesterol 0 mg

17-Sauteed Okra

Time: 25 minutes

Serve: 4

Ingredients:

- 12 oz okra, trimmed and cut
- 2 tsp lime juice
- 1/4 tsp ground turmeric
- 1/4 cup coconut, shredded
- 1/8 tsp asafetida
- 1 green chili, sliced
- 1 tbsp garlic, minced
- 1 tsp cumin seeds
- 1 tsp mustard seeds
- 1/4 cup oil
- Salt

Directions:

- Heat oil in pan over medium high heat.
- Add cumin seeds and mustard seeds and sauté for 30 seconds.
- Add garlic, asafetida, and green chili and sauté for 30 seconds.
- Add okra and stir well. Season with salt.
- Cook okra until tender about 10 minutes.
- Add turmeric and coconut and stir well.
- Remove from heat and stir in lemon juice.
- Serve hot and enjoy.

Nutritional Value (Amount per Serving):

- Calories 182
- Fat 15.9 g
- Carbohydrates 8.6 g
- Sugar 1.7 g
- Protein 2.3 g
- Cholesterol 0 mg

18-Chicken Korma

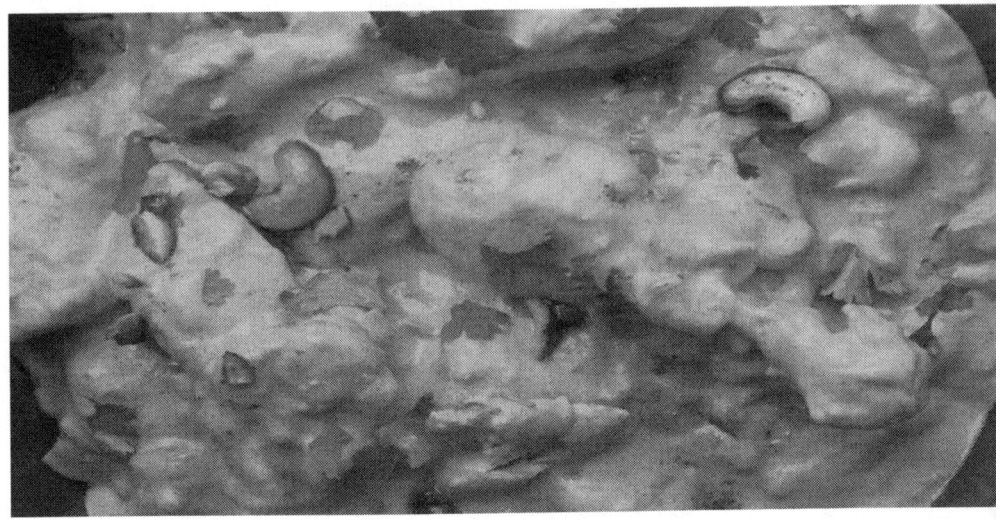

Time: 35 minutes

Serve: 4

Ingredients:

- 1 1/2 lbs chicken breast, boneless, skinless and cut into pieces
- 1/4 cup fresh cilantro, chopped
- 2/3 cup plain yogurt
- 1/2 cup water
- 8 oz can tomato sauce
- 1/8 tsp cardamom
- 1 tsp curry powder
- 1 tsp turmeric
- 1 tsp paprika
- 1 tsp sugar
- 2 tsp coriander
- 2 tsp cumin
- 2 tsp garlic, minced
- 2 tsp fresh ginger, minced

- 1 1/2 cups onion, minced
- 3 tbsp oil
- 1/2 cup heavy cream
- 1/2 cup can coconut milk
- 1/4 cup cashews
- 1 tsp salt

Directions:

- Add cream, coconut milk, and cashews in blender and blend until smooth. Set aside.
- Heat oil in pan over medium heat.
- Add onion and ginger and sauté for 3 minutes.
- Add garlic and sauté for 2 minutes.
- Add chicken, salt, and spices and sauté for 3 minutes.
- Add little amount of water if spices stick to pan.
- Stir in water and tomato sauce. Bring to boil over medium high heat.
- Cover and reduce heat to low and simmer for 10 minutes.
- Turn off the heat and allow to sit for 5 minutes.
- Stir in cream mixture.
- Turn heat to medium and cook for 20 minutes or until thicken.
- Garnish with cilantro and serve.

Nutritional Value (Amount per Serving):

- Calories 519
- Fat 31.1 g
- Carbohydrates 17.6 g
- Sugar 8.7 g
- Protein 42.4 g
- Cholesterol 132 mg

19-Spinach Lentil Soup

Time: 30 minutes

Serve: 2

Ingredients:

- 1/2 cup red lentils, rinsed and drained
- 1 cup spinach, chopped
- 2 1/2 cups water
- 1/3 tsp cayenne
- 1/2 tsp ground turmeric
- 1/8 tsp fenugreek seeds
- 1/3 tsp cumin seeds
- 1/2 tsp mustard seeds
- 1 tsp oil
- 2/3 tsp salt

Directions:

- Heat oil in a saucepan over medium heat.
- Add whole spices in pan and mix well.
- Add cayenne and turmeric and give quick stir.
- Add lentils and stir for minute.
- Add salt and water and stir well.
- Cover and cook for 20 minutes or until lentil cooked.
- Add spinach and stir well.
- Adjust seasoning and simmer for 2 minutes.
- Serve hot and enjoy.

Nutritional Value (Amount per Serving):

- Calories 202
- Fat 3.3 g
- Carbohydrates 30.5 g
- Sugar 1.2 g
- Protein 13.2 g
- Cholesterol 0 mg

20-Spicy Egg Keema

Time: 30 minutes

Serve: 2

Ingredients:

- 2 eggs, boiled and chopped
- 1 tsp cayenne
- 10 curry leaves
- 1/2 tsp cumin seeds
- 4 tbsp oil
- 1/2 tsp salt
- 1/2 tsp garam masala
- 1 tsp coriander powder
- 1 tsp ginger garlic paste
- 1 tomato
- 1 cup onion

Directions:

- Heat oil in a pan over medium heat.
- Add cumin seeds, green chilies, onion, and curry leaves and cook until onion soften.
- Add ginger garlic paste and cook for minute.
- Add tomato and cook until soften.
- Add cayenne, salt, coriander powder, and turmeric powder and stir well.
- Add salt and garam masala and mix well.
- Now add chopped eggs and stir well.
- Serve hot and enjoy.

Nutritional Value (Amount per Serving):

- Calories 337
- Fat 32 g
- Carbohydrates 7.7 g
- Sugar 3.7 g
- Protein 6.7 g
- Cholesterol 164 mg

SNACK RECIPES
21-Roasted Chickpeas

Time: 50 minutes

Serve: 6

Ingredients:

- 4 cups chickpeas, cooked
- 1 tsp garam masala
- 1/2 tsp garlic powder
- 2 tsp cumin
- 2 tsp red chili powder
- 4 tbsp olive oil
- Salt

Directions:

- Preheat the oven to 400 F.

- Place cooked chickpeas on roasting tray and drizzle with 2 tbsp olive oil and season with salt. Mix well.
- Roast in preheated oven for 30 minutes.
- Reduce temperature to 175 F and roast for 30 minutes.
- After 30 minutes sprinkle with all spices and toss well return in oven for 4 minutes.
- Let the cool completely then serve.

Nutritional Value (Amount per Serving):

- Calories 571
- Fat 17.7 g
- Carbohydrates 81.8 g
- Sugar 14.4 g
- Protein 26 g
- Cholesterol 0 mg

22-Corn Patties

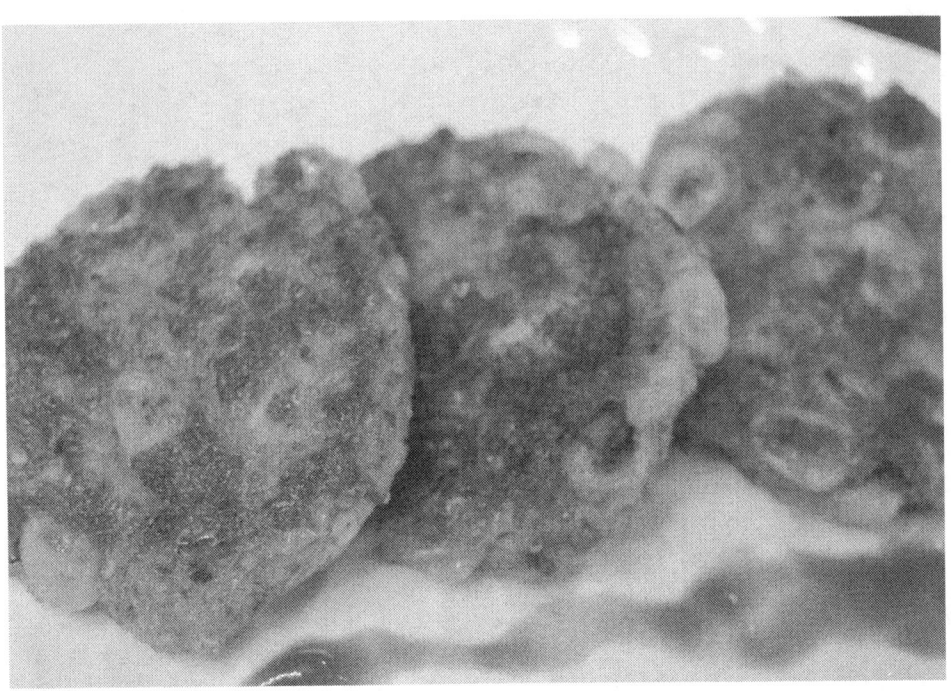

Time: 30 minutes

Serve: 8

Ingredients:

- 3/4 cup sweet corn, boil
- 1 cup potatoes, boil
- 2 tbsp oil
- 1/4 cup bread crumbs
- 1/2 tsp ginger paste
- 1/2 tsp garam masala
- 1/2 tsp red chili powder
- 2 tbsp coriander leaves, chopped
- 1 green chili, chopped
- Salt

Directions:

- Mash the potatoes well.
- Add remaining ingredients in mash potatoes and knead well.
- Make 8 round patties from mixture.
- Heat oil in pan over medium heat.
- Place patties on hot pan and cook until lightly golden brown from both the sides.
- Serve with sauce and enjoy.

Nutritional Value (Amount per Serving):

- Calories 70
- Fat 3.8 g
- Carbohydrates 8.3 g
- Sugar 0.9 g
- Protein 1.3 g
- Cholesterol 0 mg

23-Crispy Cauliflower Pakoda

Time: 25 minutes

Serve: 4

Ingredients:

- 3 cups cauliflower florets
- 1/4 cup rice flour
- 7 tbsp gram flour
- 1 tsp garam masala
- 1 tsp red chili powder
- 1 1/2 tsp carom seeds
- 1 1/4 tsp ginger garlic paste
- 2 green chilies, chopped
- Salt
- Oil for frying

Directions:

- Add cauliflower into hot salted water and leave for sometime then drain well.
- Add drained cauliflower florets into the mixing bowl.
- Add all remaining ingredients and mix well.
- Sprinkle water and coat cauliflower well with flour mixture. Use water as needed.
- Heat oil in pan.
- Once oil is hot then add coated cauliflower florets into the oil and fry until golden on medium heat.
- Drain on paper towel and serve hot.

Nutritional Value (Amount per Serving):

- Calories 96
- Fat 1 g
- Carbohydrates 18.1 g
- Sugar 3 g
- Protein 4.4 g
- Cholesterol 0 mg

24-Tasty Garlic Paneer

Time: 15 minutes

Serve: 2

Ingredients:

- 1 1/4 cup paneer
- 1/2 cup onion, chopped
- 1/2 tsp cumin
- 1 tbsp oil
- 1 tsp sugar
- 5 red chilies, remove seeds
- 1 tsp vinegar
- 6 garlic cloves
- Salt

Directions:

- Add chilies, vinegar, salt, sugar, garlic, and 2 tbsp water in blender and blend until smooth.
- Heat oil in pan over medium heat.
- Add cumin and sauté for minute.
- Add onion and sauté until lightly golden brown.
- Add chilies mixture and cook until thicken.
- Add paneer and sauté for 3 minutes.
- Serve hot and enjoy.

Nutritional Value (Amount per Serving):

- Calories 173
- Fat 7 g
- Carbohydrates 18.4 g
- Sugar 15.3 g
- Protein 8.5 g
- Cholesterol 5 mg

25-Sweet Corn Fritters

Time: 25 minutes

Serve: 4

Ingredients:

- 1 1/2 cups can sweet corn, drained
- 1/2 tsp red chili powder
- 2 green chilies
- 1 small onion, sliced
- 1/2 tsp garam masala
- 2 tbsp rice flour
- 2 tbsp gram flour
- 1/2 tsp cumin
- 1 tsp ginger garlic paste
- 1/8 tsp turmeric powder
- Salt

- Oil for frying

Directions:

- Add corn in food processor and process until coarsely. Transfer in bowl.
- Add remaining ingredients and mix well to combine.
- Heat oil in deep pan.
- Once oil is hot then drop small portions of corn mixture to hot oil and fry until golden and crisp.
- Drain them on paper towel.
- Serve hot with sauce and enjoy.

Nutritional Value (Amount per Serving):

- Calories 88
- Fat 1 g
- Carbohydrates 19.1 g
- Sugar 3 g
- Protein 2.8 g
- Cholesterol 0 mg

26-Stir Fried Cumin Potato

Time: 20 minutes

Serve: 2

Ingredients:

- 3 medium potatoes, boiled and cubed
- 1 tbsp cilantro, chopped
- 1 tbsp lemon juice
- 1/4 tsp red chili powder
- 1 green chili, chopped
- 1/4 tsp turmeric powder
- 1 tsp coriander seeds, crushed
- 2 tsp cumin seeds
- 2 tbsp vegetable oil
- Salt

Directions:

- Heat oil in pan over medium heat.
- Add cumin wait till cumin seed crackle.
- Add green chili and coriander seeds and sauté for minutes.
- Add red chili powder and turmeric powder and stir well.
- Add potatoes and stir well.
- Season with salt and cook for another 2 minutes over medium heat.
- Remove from heat and add lemon juice and mix well.
- Serve hot and enjoy.

Nutritional Value (Amount per Serving):

- Calories 353
- Fat 14.5 g
- Carbohydrates 51.7 g
- Sugar 3.9 g
- Protein 5.9 g
- Cholesterol 0 mg

27-Cucumber Tomato Onion Salad

Time: 15 minutes

Serve: 4

Ingredients:

- 1 large cucumber, chopped
- 2 medium tomatoes, chopped
- 1 small onion, chopped
- 1 tsp lemon juice
- 1/4 tsp cayenne
- 1/4 cup cilantro, chopped
- 1 green chili, chopped
- 1/4 tsp ground black pepper
- 1/4 tsp salt

Directions:

- Add all ingredients into the mixing bowl and toss well.
- Serve and enjoy.

Nutritional Value (Amount per Serving):

- Calories 31
- Fat 0.3 g
- Carbohydrates 7 g
- Sugar 3.7 g
- Protein 1.3 g
- Cholesterol 0 mg

28-Sweet and Spicy Carrot Peas Stir Fry

Time: 20 minutes

Serve: 4

Ingredients:

- 2 large carrots, peeled and chopped
- 1 tbsp coriander leaves
- 1/4 tsp dry mango powder
- 1 tsp coriander powder
- 1/4 tsp turmeric
- 1/2 tsp red chili powder
- 1/2 tsp cumin seeds
- 1 tbsp oil
- 1/2 cup peas
- Salt

Directions:

- Heat oil in pan over medium heat.
- Add cumin seeds and stir for minute.
- Add peas and carrots and reduce heat to low.
- Add turmeric and salt and stir well. Cover and cook for 10 minutes.
- When peas and carrots and half cooked then add chili powder and coriander powder.
- Cover again and cook until peas and carrots turn soft.
- Now add chopped coriander and mango powder and mix well.
- Serve hot and enjoy.

Nutritional Value (Amount per Serving):

- Calories 62
- Fat 3.6 g
- Carbohydrates 6.6 g
- Sugar 2.8 g
- Protein 1.4 g
- Cholesterol 0 mg

29-Coconut Rice

Time: 30 minutes

Serve: 4

Ingredients:

- 1 cup rice
- 1/4 cup cilantro, chopped
- 2 tbsp scallions, chopped
- 1/4 cup water
- 1/2 tsp kosher salt
- 1 tbsp lime juice
- 1 lemon zest
- 14 oz can coconut milk
- 1/4 cup slivered almonds

Directions:

- In a pan toast almonds until lightly golden brown and set aside.
- In a saucepan add all ingredients including toasted almonds and stir well.
- Cover pan with lid and simmer on low for 15 minutes.
- Remove saucepan from heat and set aside for 5 minutes.
- Using fork fluff the rice and serve.

Nutritional Value (Amount per Serving):

- Calories 400
- Fat 24.5 g
- Carbohydrates 41.3 g
- Sugar 0.4 g
- Protein 6.6 g
- Cholesterol 0 mg

30-Coconut Turmeric Rice

Time: 25 minutes

Serve: 6

Ingredients:

- 1 cup basmati rice, rinsed and drained
- 1 1/4 cup water
- 7 oz coconut milk
- 1 1/2 tsp ground turmeric
- 1 tbsp ginger, grated
- 3 garlic cloves, minced
- 1/2 onion, diced
- 1 1/2 tbsp olive oil
- 1/2 tsp salt

Directions:

- Heat olive oil in a saucepan over medium heat.

- Add onion, ginger, garlic and salt and sauté for 5 minutes.
- Add turmeric and rice and stir well.
- Add water and coconut milk and stir to combine. Bring to boil.
- Cover and reduce heat to low and cook for 18 minutes or until all liquid absorbed.
- Using fork fluff the rice and serve.

Nutritional Value (Amount per Serving):

- Calories 230
- Fat 11.7 g
- Carbohydrates 28.8 g
- Sugar 1.6 g
- Protein 3.3 g
- Cholesterol 0 mg

SALAD RECIPES
31-Spicy Cabbage Salad

Time: 20 minutes

Serve: 4

Ingredients:

- 1/2 small cabbage, shredded
- 1 carrot, peeled and cut into strips
- 1 chili, sliced
- 1/2 tsp turmeric
- 1 tsp mustard seeds
- 1 tbsp oil
- 1/2 tsp salt

Directions:

- Heat oil in large pan over medium heat.

- Add mustard seeds and stir for minute.
- Reduce heat to low and add turmeric and chili and cook for minute.
- Add carrot, cabbage and salt and stir over medium heat for 5 minutes.
- Serve immediately and enjoy.

Nutritional Value (Amount per Serving):

- Calories 64
- Fat 3.8 g
- Carbohydrates 7.2 g
- Sugar 3.7 g
- Protein 1.5 g
- Cholesterol 0 mg

32-Spicy Chickpea Salad

Time: 20 minutes

Serve: 4

Ingredients:

- 2 cups chickpeas, rinsed and drained
- 1/4 cup cilantro, minced
- 1/4 cup onion, sliced
- 1 1/2 cups cherry tomato, sliced
- 1 1/2 cups cucumber, chopped
- 1 tbsp lemon juice
- 1/2 tsp lemon zest
- 1/4 tsp ground cumin
- 1 tbsp olive oil
- Salt

Directions:

- Heat olive oil in pan over medium heat.
- Add cumin and chickpeas with spices and stir well.
- Cook chickpeas until lightly golden brown then remove from heat.
- Now combine together all remaining ingredients into the mixing bowl.
- Add roasted chickpeas and toss well.
- Serve and enjoy.

Nutritional Value (Amount per Serving):

- Calories 405
- Fat 9.7 g
- Carbohydrates 63 g
- Sugar 11.8 g
- Protein 19.7 g
- Cholesterol 0 mg

33-Yogurt Cucumber Salad

Time: 20 minutes

Serve: 4

Ingredients:

- 2 large cucumbers, sliced
- 1 garlic clove, grated
- 2 tbsp dill, chopped
- 1 lemon juice
- 1/4 cup yogurt
- 1/4 cup onion, sliced
- Pepper
- Salt

Directions:

- Add all ingredients into the bowl and mix well.

- Serve immediately and enjoy.

Nutritional Value (Amount per Serving):

- Calories 47
- Fat 1 g
- Carbohydrates 63 g
- Sugar 8 g
- Protein 2 g
- Cholesterol 2 mg

34-Healthy Kidney Bean Salad

Time: 15 minutes

Serve: 2

Ingredients:

- 1/2 cup kidney beans, soak in water for 8 hours
- 2 tbsp peanuts, roasted and crushed
- 2 tsp olive oil
- 3 tsp lemon juice
- 2 tbsp coriander, chopped
- 2 tsp green chili, chopped
- 1 cup onion, chopped

Directions:

- Drain kidney beans well and add into the pressure cooker.

- Add salt and 3 cups water and stir well.
- Cover pressure cooker and cook until soften.
- Drain beans well and add in mixing bowl.
- Add all remaining ingredients and toss well.
- Serve and enjoy.

Nutritional Value (Amount per Serving):

- Calories 274
- Fat 9.8 g
- Carbohydrates 35.6 g
- Sugar 4.1 g
- Protein 13.4 g
- Cholesterol 0 mg

35-Yogurt Cucumber Tomato Salad

Time: 10 minutes

Serve: 2

Ingredients:

- 1/3 cup yogurt
- 1 large tomatoes, seeded and diced
- 1 large cucumber, seeded and diced
- 1/4 cup fresh cilantro, chopped
- 1/2 tsp sugar
- 1/4 tsp cumin
- 1 tbsp lemon juice
- 1 small onion, diced
- 1 large sweet pepper, diced
- Pepper
- Salt

Directions:

- Add cucumber, onion, tomatoes, and pepper in bowl and set aside.
- In small bowl, whisk together sugar, lemon juice, yogurt, cumin, pepper, and salt.
- Pour dressing over vegetables and mix well.
- Serve and enjoy.

Nutritional Value (Amount per Serving):

- Calories 108
- Fat 1.2 g
- Carbohydrates 21 g
- Sugar 13.4 g
- Protein 5.3 g
- Cholesterol 2 mg

DESSERT RECIPES
36-Fruit Custard

Time: 25 minutes

Serve: 6

Ingredients:

- 2 1/2 cups milk
- 1/4 tsp vanilla essence
- 2 1/2 tbsp custard powder
- 6 tbsp sugar
- 4 cups fruits, chopped

Directions:

- Add milk in a saucepan and bring to simmer.
- Remove 1/4 cup warm milk and mix custard powder in it.

- Add custard and milk mixture into the boiling milk and mix well.
- Add vanilla essence and sugar and stir over low heat.
- Stir milk and custard mixture continuously to avoid lumps and cook until thickens.
- Remove from heat and allow to cool completely.
- Add chopped fruits and stir well.
- Pour into the serving glasses and place in refrigerator.
- Serve chilled and enjoy.

Nutritional Value (Amount per Serving):

- Calories 101
- Fat 2.1 g
- Carbohydrates 18.1 g
- Sugar 16.6 g
- Protein 3.4 g
- Cholesterol 8 mg

37-Sweet Mango Coconut Fudge

Time: 35 minutes

Serve: 12

Ingredients:

- 1/2 cup mango puree
- 1 1/2 cups coconut, grated
- 5 pistachios, chopped
- 1/8 tsp cardamom powder
- 1/3 cup sugar
- 1/2 cup milk

Directions:

- Grease the baking tray with butter.
- Add coconut in pan and roast over medium heat until lightly brown.

- Add mango puree, sugar, and milk.
- Mix well and cook over medium heat until mixture thickens it takes about 20 minutes. Stir continuously.
- Remove pan from heat and add cardamom powder and mix well.
- Pour mixture into the grease tray and spread evenly.
- Sprinkle chopped pistachios on top and press lightly.
- Let the fudge mixture cool completely then cut into pieces and serve.

Nutritional Value (Amount per Serving):

- Calories 70
- Fat 3.6 g
- Carbohydrates 9.7 g
- Sugar 8.6 g
- Protein 0.8 g
- Cholesterol 1 mg

38-Easy Milk Powder Fudge

Time: 20 minutes

Serve: 6

Ingredients:

- 1 cup milk powder
- 1/4 cup butter
- 1/4 cup milk
- 1/2 cup powdered sugar

Directions:

- Grease tray with butter.
- Heat butter in pan over low heat.
- Add milk powder and milk and stir well.
- Add powdered sugar and stir continuously and cook until mixture thickens.

- Pour mixture into the grease tray and spread evenly.
- Allow it to cool completely then cut into pieces and serve.

Nutritional Value (Amount per Serving):

- Calories 192
- Fat 7.9 g
- Carbohydrates 22 g
- Sugar 20.9 g
- Protein 8.4 g
- Cholesterol 25 mg

39-Fresh Carrot Halwa

Time: 55 minutes

Serve: 10

Ingredients:

- 2 lbs fresh carrots, peeled and grated
- 2 tbsp raisins
- 7 almonds, soaked and sliced
- 2 tsp cardamom powder
- 2 tbsp butter
- 1/2 cup milk
- 1/2 cup sweetened condensed milk

Directions:

- Melt butter in a heavy bottom pan over medium heat.
- Add grated carrots and sauté until tender.

- Add milk, condensed milk, almonds, and raisins. Mix well.
- Cover and cook over medium low heat until it dries.
- Remove from heat and add cardamom powder and stir well.
- Serve warm and enjoy.

Nutritional Value (Amount per Serving):

- Calories 124
- Fat 4.3 g
- Carbohydrates 19.7 g
- Sugar 14.4 g
- Protein 2.7 g
- Cholesterol 12 mg

40-Delicious Indian Malai Ladoo

Time: 35 minutes

Serve: 15

Ingredients:

- 8 cups whole milk
- 1 tsp cardamom powder
- 14 oz sweetened condensed milk
- 1/4 cup vinegar

Directions:

- Add milk in a saucepan and bring to boil.
- Add vinegar 2 to 3 times until curd forms.
- Separates curd from the whey and rinse well in cold water.
- Squeeze out all liquid from curd and knead curd until get smooth texture.

- In a pan add curd, cardamom powder, and condensed milk and mix well and cook over medium heat until mixture thickens.
- Once mixture is thick then remove from heat and allow to cool completely.
- Make small round shape ball from mixture and serve.

Nutritional Value (Amount per Serving):

- Calories 164
- Fat 6.5 g
- Carbohydrates 20.4 g
- Sugar 21.3 g
- Protein 6.3 g
- Cholesterol 22 mg

If you enjoyed this book or received value from it in any way, then I'd like to ask you for a favor: would you be kind enough to leave a review for this book on Amazon? It'd be greatly appreciated!

Thank you and good luck!

Made in the USA
Lexington, KY
12 October 2017